Depression

An information guide

REVISED EDITION

Christina Bartha, MSW, RSW
Carol Parker, MSW, RSW
Cathy Thomson, MSW, RSW
Kate Kitchen, MSW, RSW

camh
Centre for Addiction and Mental Health

Library and Archives Canada Cataloguing in Publication

Depression : an information guide / Christina Bartha, Carol Parker, Cathy Thomson, Kate Kitchen. -- Revised edition.

Includes bibliographical references.
Issued in print and electronic formats.

ISBN: 978-1-77052-571-9 (PRINT)
ISBN: 978-1-77052-572-6 (PDF)
ISBN: 978-1-77052-573-3 (HTML)
ISBN: 978-1-77052-574-0 (EPUB)

I. Depression, Mental--Popular works. I. Bartha, Christina, author
II. Centre for Addiction and Mental Health, issuing body

RC537.D456 2013   616.85'27   C2013-905654-8
                                            C2013-905655-6

Printed in Canada
Copyright © 1999, 2008, 2013 Centre for Addiction and Mental Health

This publication may be available in other formats. For information about alternate formats or other CAMH publications, or to place an order, please contact Sales and Distribution:
Toll-free: 1 800 661-1111
Toronto: 416 595-6059
E-mail: publications@camh.ca
Online store: http://store.camh.ca

Website: www.camh.ca

Disponible en français sous le titre :
La dépression : Guide d'information

This guide was produced by CAMH's Knowledge and Innovation Support Unit.

3973e / 01-2014 / PM103

Contents

Acknowledgments

The authors would like to acknowledge the assistance of Drs. Sid Kennedy and Joel Raskin, whose review of and comments on the section on medications in the first edition were very helpful. We would also like to thank Tom and Meg for their invaluable thoughtfulness and assistance in reviewing this publication from the perspective of a patient/consumer and family member.

This revised edition was reviewed by Frances Abela-Dimech, BScN, MN, CPMHN(C), and Claudia Tindall, MSW, RSW.

Introduction

This guide is for people living with depression, their families and anyone who wants to understand the basics of this illness and its treatment and management. It is not a substitute for treatment from a doctor or mental health care provider, but it can be used as a basis for questions and discussion about depression. This handbook covers many aspects of depression and answers frequently asked questions. With respect to treating depression, new therapies and medications are continually being developed and some current medications may not have been available when this guide was published.

1 Understanding depression

"Depression is such cruel punishment. There are no fevers, no rashes, no blood tests to send people scurrying with concern. Just the slow erosion of the self, as insidious as any cancer. And, like cancer, it is essentially a solitary experience. A room in hell with only your name on the door. I realize that every person, at some point, takes up residence in one or other of these rooms. But the realization offers no great comfort now."

—Martha Manning, Undercurrents (1994)
author/therapist who has dealt with major depression

The pain and isolation of depression, a psychiatric illness, is difficult for many people to understand. Depression is a word that is used both for a sad, despairing mood and for a psychiatric disorder. Everyone feels sad, down or blue at times, often following a disappointment, loss of a loved one or other traumatic life event. This is a normal reaction and our depressed moods usually lift fairly quickly. Sometimes, though, a depressed mood can persist and become a more significant mental health problem, commonly referred to as clinical or major depression.

What is major depression?

Depression is much worse than simple unhappiness. Major depression (also called clinical depression) is a **mood disorder**. This means that a person's emotional state is abnormally low or sad, and the person cannot independently raise his or her mood. The chief symptom of major depression is a sad, despairing mood that persists beyond two weeks and impairs a person's performance at work, at school or in social relationships. This profoundly low mood state can be confusing because some of the symptoms of depression are behavioural, such as moving or talking slowly, while others are emotional and cognitive, such as feeling hopeless and thinking negative thoughts. This is very different from the physical symptoms of other illnesses, like the pain of a broken leg or the fever from a serious infection.

Depression is more common in women, though the sex difference diminishes with increasing age in Canada. Depression is most common in people between the ages of 15 and 45.

HOW IS DEPRESSION DIAGNOSED?

In making a diagnosis, a doctor will ask you if you have experienced any of the following:

• changes in appetite and weight
• sleep problems, either sleeping too much or too little
• loss of interest in work, hobbies, people; loss of feeling for family members and friends
• feelings of uselessness, hopelessness, excessive guilt
• preoccupation with failure(s) or inadequacies and a loss of self-esteem; certain thoughts that are obsessional and difficult to "turn off"

- agitation or loss of energy; feelings of restlessness, or being too tired and weak to do anything
- slowed thinking, forgetfulness, trouble concentrating and making decisions
- decreased sexual drive
- a tendency to cry easily, or having the urge to cry but being unable to do so
- suicidal or occasionally homicidal thoughts
- in some cases, a loss of touch with reality, perhaps hearing voices (hallucinations) or having strange ideas (delusions).

Depressive disorders can vary in severity. A person who experiences fewer than five of the symptoms of major depression for two weeks or more is diagnosed with minor depression. When someone experiences five or more of these typical symptoms for at least two weeks, this is called a "major depressive episode." For many people, however, their struggle with depression has persisted for weeks, months or even years before they visit a doctor or mental health care provider. It is not uncommon for people to try to cope on their own while feeling their mood "slipping" or "dropping," until it reaches a point that feels intolerable. People struggling with depression may also find themselves to be much more sensitive to comments from others, and they get little or no relief when loved ones and friends try to cheer them up or offer support.

The length of a depressive episode is influenced by the person's ability or willingness to get treatment. A treated depressive episode may only last for two to six weeks; however, untreated episodes may last six to 18 months or longer. The average is about five months.

DEPRESSION AND BIPOLAR DISORDER

Depression also occurs in **bipolar disorder** (formerly known as manic-depressive illness). Bipolar disorder is a mood disorder, but is characterized by episodes of **mania** as well as episodes of depression. A person with mania will typically have an inflated or grandiose perception of his or her own importance or power. This can result in excessive involvement in activities that can lead to painful consequences (e.g., foolish business investments, shopping sprees, sexual indiscretions). People with mania may also have less need for sleep, a pattern of very rapid speech and racing thoughts. During a manic episode, many people are unaware that their behaviour is unusual. Before a manic episode, however, people generally experience a **hypomanic phase**, where they exhibit some less severe symptoms of mania (e.g., sleep disruption, a racing feeling), and are aware that they may be heading toward a full manic episode. This insight allows them to seek medical intervention and possibly avert a full-blown manic episode.

While they share similar symptoms of depression, bipolar disorder and major depression are separate disorders requiring different treatment. Because of this, it is important for patients, family members and health care providers to watch for signs of mania or hypomania in people experiencing depression. Other warning signs for the presence of bipolar disorder include:

• depression that begins in the teenage years
• certain kinds of depression (**atypical depression**, seasonal depression, postpartum depression, and possibly depression with psychosis), whose symptoms may all sometimes occur as part of bipolar disorder.

Different kinds of depression

Major depression is broken down into subtypes, each with a slightly different set of symptoms. It is important to receive an accurate diagnosis, because different types of depression may respond better to different types of treatments.

DEPRESSION WITH TYPICAL OR ATYPICAL FEATURES

In addition to the general features of depression, people with typical symptoms of depression tend to experience sleep difficulties (trouble falling asleep, sleeping less than usual, and/or frequent waking through the night), decreased appetite, and weight loss.

People with **atypical symptoms** share the general features of major depression, but some symptoms are reversed: they tend to *over*sleep, eat *more* than normal and *gain* weight. In addition:

• symptoms of **anxiety** are often present
• evening rather than morning tends to be the hardest part of the day
• arms or legs may feel heavy and leaden
• the person may be highly sensitive to feelings of rejection (even when not feeling depressed).

While a person with typical symptoms is generally unresponsive, atypical depression is characterized by "mood reactivity." This means that a person will be able to respond positively to something good or a pleasurable event, such as a visit from a relative, but will quickly become depressed again when the source of this pleasure disappears. These shifts up and down can be very difficult both for the person and for family members.

Atypical depression tends to be more common in teenagers and young adults.

SEASONAL AFFECTIVE DISORDER (SEASONAL DEPRESSION)

Seasonal affective disorder (SAD) is a type of depression in which mood tends to be affected by the weather and time of the year. Symptoms usually occur during the fall and winter, and the person feels better during the spring and summer. People struggling with SAD usually experience several symptoms, including several-months-long sad mood, increased sleep and increased appetite, characterized by carbohydrate cravings and weight gain. Women experience SAD four times more than men.

SAD is more common in northern climates, where there is a significant decrease in the hours of sunlight over the winter months. It is not unusual for anyone to experience some changes in mood during periods of decreased sunlight. However, people with SAD will experience much more severe symptoms that interfere with their ability to work and relate well to others, though the symptoms of SAD are generally less severe than those of major depression.

POSTPARTUM DEPRESSION

While all types of depression may have multiple causes, **postpartum depression** follows a specific event, the birth of a child. Its onset may be related to biochemical and hormonal changes, emotional issues and social circumstances. Upwards of 10 per cent of women will experience this type of depression, which is characterized by the major symptoms of depression that persist for four weeks or more and interfere with a mother's social and emotional functioning. Postpartum depression differs from the more common and less severe post-partum blues, which many women experience after childbirth.

Women who have had depressive episodes before pregnancy may be more vulnerable to developing a postpartum depression. Emotional issues, such as whether the baby was planned or unplanned, or whether the mother has support from the father and extended family, may also contribute to the onset of a depression. The responsibility of a new infant combined with the symptoms of depression can make this a very difficult time socially. Family and friends may wonder how the mother of a new baby could not be feeling joy on such a happy occasion. This may make the new mother experiencing depression feel more isolated and uncomfortable in coming forward to ask for help.

DEPRESSION WITH PSYCHOSIS

In some cases, depression may become so severe that a person loses touch with reality and becomes psychotic. Psychosis involves a break with reality in which a person experiences **hallucinations** (hearing voices or seeing people or objects that are not really there) or **delusions** (beliefs that have no basis in reality). Delusions may be paranoid, such as when the person believes that others are plotting against him or her. Hallucinations and delusions may be very critical or negative, and this may make the depressive state worse. When a person with depression also has psychotic symptoms, treatment involves both antidepressant and antipsychotic medications.

DYSTHYMIA

Dysthymia, or **dysthymic disorder**, describes a chronically low mood with some moderate symptoms of depression, such as poor appetite or overeating, inability to sleep or sleeping too much, low energy or fatigue, low self-esteem, poor concentration, difficulty making decisions and feelings of hopelessness. If two or more of these symptoms last for two or more years, and a person does not experience a major depressive episode during this time, then a diagnosis of dysthymia may be made. While not as severe as major depression, dysthymia can interfere with a person's functioning at work, at school or in important relationships. A person may have dysthymia, and then experience a major depressive episode. This is known as **double depression.**

Personality disorders and depression

Sometimes, people with depression may also be told by a doctor or psychologist that they have a **personality disorder.** What does this mean, and how does it affect the depression? Personality is what makes up the whole of the person, including thoughts, feelings, actions and relationships with others. A personality trait refers to the identifiable patterns of individuals; their usual ways of thinking and feeling, their habitual behaviours and their characteristic ways of relating to others.

A personality disorder is a statement about the person's personality traits. It means that the person is seen to have patterns of thoughts and feelings, behaviours and relationship styles that differ in significant ways from the culture in which he or she lives. Not only do these patterns differ from the norm, but they also lead the person to feel bad about himself or herself and interfere with his or her ability to function well at work and in his or her personal life.

A person will be diagnosed with a specific type of personality disorder. For example, a person diagnosed as having a paranoid personality disorder will have problems trusting others in most parts of his or her life, even when there is no basis for suspicions. This pervasive distrust complicates the treatment of depression, because it interferes with the person's ability to develop and maintain relationships with others who might be able to provide needed support, including a doctor or mental health care provider.

Many people have some of these personality characteristics, without any significant interference in their lives. For example, if someone is slow to trust, but is able to gain a belief in the goodwill of one or two friends or family members over time, we would think of this quality as being a personality trait, but not one that keeps the person from engaging in a satisfying life. This person would not be diagnosed as having a personality disorder.

Other examples of personality disorders are schizoid (great difficulty attaching emotionally to others), borderline (a pattern of unstable relationships, with impulsive and sometimes self-destructive behaviour), and obsessive-compulsive (perfectionist, focused on minute details to the exclusion of others' thoughts and opinions). (Obsessive-compulsive *personality* disorder is different from obsessive-compulsive disorder, which is an anxiety disorder characterized by repeated unwanted thoughts and repetitive behaviours aimed at reducing anxiety.)

While personality disorders differ in how they manifest in each person, they all get in the way of people living comfortably with themselves or others. A person struggling with depression and a personality disorder not only needs to feel better, but also needs to learn new ways of relating to the world. This person's treatment will likely include both medication and **psychotherapy.**

2 What causes depression?

There is no simple answer to what causes depression, because several factors may play a part in the onset of the disorder. These include a genetic or family history of depression, psychological or emotional vulnerability to depression, biological factors, and life event or environmental stressors. The fact that you may be undertaking one type of treatment, for example antidepressant medication, does not mean your depression is entirely biological. What it does mean is that often depression can be effectively treated by focusing on one area, such as the biochemistry in the brain. The type of treatment recommended is also often influenced by the severity of your depression. If someone is severely depressed, it is difficult for the person to undertake the "talking therapies." As a result, medication may be the first stage of treatment, followed by psychotherapy as a second stage of intervention. Once you are feeling somewhat better, you may be better able to tolerate talking about other life problems that contribute to your depression.

Everyone has a certain number of "risk" or "vulnerability" factors. The more risk factors a person has, and the greater the level of stress on the person, the greater the chance of having a depressive episode. This is known as the stress-vulnerability model.

The stress-vulnerability model—risk factors in depression

GENETIC AND FAMILY HISTORY

A family history of depression does not necessarily mean that children or other relatives will develop major depression. However, people with a family history of depression have a slightly higher chance of becoming depressed at some stage in their lives. There are several theories to explain this phenomenon.

Genetic research suggests that depression can run in families. Studies of twins raised separately have shown that if one twin develops the disorder, the other has a 40 to 50 per cent chance of also being affected. This rate, though it is moderate, suggests that some people may have a genetic predisposition to developing depression.

A genetic predisposition alone, however, is unlikely to cause depression. Other factors, such as traumatic childhood or adult life events, may act as triggers. The onset of depression may also be influenced by what we learn as children. Some people may have been exposed to the depressive symptoms of their parents and have learned this as a way of reacting to certain problems. As adults, they may go on to use these strategies to deal with their own life stressors. Growing up with one parent who has been depressed puts a child at a 10 per cent risk of developing the disorder. If both parents were depressed, there is a 30 per cent risk. *These figures are lower than those for other types of illness that may be passed on from parent to child.*

If you have a family history of depression, it is important to educate yourself about the disorder and what you can do to protect yourself against it.

PSYCHOLOGICAL VULNERABILITY

Personality style, and the way you have learned to deal with problems, may contribute to the onset of depression. If you are the type of person who has a low opinion of yourself and worries a lot, if you are overly dependent on others, if you are a perfectionist and expect too much from yourself or others, or if you tend to hide your feelings, you may be at greater risk of becoming depressed.

LIFE EVENTS OR ENVIRONMENTAL STRESSES

Some studies suggest that early childhood trauma and losses— such as the death or separation of parents—or adult life events— such as the death of a loved one, divorce, the loss of a job, retirement, serious financial problems, or family conflict—can lead to the onset of depression. Experiencing several severe and prolonged difficult life events increases a person's chances of developing a depressive disorder. Once depressed, it is common for a person to remember earlier traumatic life events, such as the loss of a parent or childhood abuse, which make the depression worse.

Living with chronic family problems can also seriously affect a person's mood and lead to depressive symptoms. People living in emotionally abusive or violent relationships can feel trapped, both financially and emotionally, and feel hopeless about their future. This is particularly true of mothers with young children. The ongoing stress and social isolation associated with these family circumstances can lead to depressive symptoms.

Once a person develops a serious depression, he or she may need intensive treatment before feeling able to deal with the situation or life stressors that triggered the onset of the illness.

BIOLOGICAL FACTORS

Depression may appear after unusual physiological changes such as childbirth, and viral or other infections. This has given rise to the theory that hormonal or chemical imbalances in the brain may cause depression. Studies have shown that there are differences in the levels of certain biochemicals between people who are depressed and those who are not. The fact that depression can be helped by antidepressant medication and brain intervention therapies tends to support this theory.

Seasonal affective disorder (SAD) is a good example of how biology and personality may work together to influence the onset of depression. Researchers are investigating whether chemicals in the brain that regulate mood, sleep and appetite are affected by changes in levels of light. Research has found that people experiencing SAD seem to be highly sensitive to their own feelings and events around them, and that these reactions are amplified by seasonal changes in light levels.

For many people with depression and their families, trying to understand the various theories that explain the onset of depression can be very confusing. While research has yet to fully explain the causes of depression, it is important to know that effective treatments are still available.

Common questions about depression

WHAT ABOUT PREMENSTRUAL SYNDROME, MENOPAUSE AND DEPRESSION?

Changes in the hormonal cycle of women have been linked with symptoms of depression. Before their monthly periods (premenstrual stage), women can experience changeable moods, irritability, anxiety, sleep difficulties, as well as abdominal cramps, bloating and breast tenderness. For women with **premenstrual tension**, these symptoms may last for a few days and then go away. For those with **premenstrual syndrome** (pms), the symptoms are more severe, and disrupt routine activities. A woman who struggles with both depression and premenstrual symptoms tends to feel much worse during this time of the month.

During **menopause**, a period of biological changes during mid-life, women must adjust to the effects of reduced levels of the hormone estrogen. The symptoms of menopause, such as hot flashes and profound sweating, may make it harder to function at work and in social situations. Menopause is also a time when women may have to deal with psychological issues and other life events—children may be leaving home, and aging spouses and family members may develop health problems. Menopause also represents the end of a woman's ability to have children. The physical and emotional stressors associated with menopause may contribute to the onset of depressive symptoms.

CAN DEPRESSION OCCUR SECONDARY TO A PHYSICAL ILLNESS?

Yes. In people with a physical illness, depression can occur in three different ways. Depressive symptoms may be the *result of another illness* that shares the same symptoms, such as lupus or hypothyroidism. Depression may be a *reaction to another illness*, such as cancer or a heart attack. Finally, depression may be *caused by an illness itself*, such as a stroke, where neurological changes have occurred. Regardless of the cause, depression in people with a physical illness is often treated with antidepressants and other therapies.

IS DEPRESSION TREATED DIFFERENTLY IN OLDER ADULTS?

Yes. Generally, older adults are given lower dosages of antidepressants because they are more sensitive to medication, prone to confusion, and may have more trouble tolerating side-effects. Potential drug interactions must be considered, because older patients are often also taking medication for other medical problems.

HOW DO ALCOHOL, STREET DRUGS AND PRESCRIPTION DRUGS INFLUENCE DEPRESSION?

Alcohol, street drugs and some prescription medications can provide a temporary break from some of the symptoms of depression. However, this "self-medication" simply *masks*—and sometimes *worsens*—the symptoms of depression, which resurface when the substance use stops. In some people, depression can be *triggered* by abuse of alcohol and other drugs. In both cases, the substance abuse itself can lead to further health problems and can disrupt a person's ability to function. In most cases, treatment for the substance abuse is given first. If the depression persists, then the mood disorder becomes the focus of intervention.

CAN PEOPLE DIAGNOSED WITH DEPRESSION ALSO EXPERIENCE ANXIETY?

Yes. As many as two-thirds of people with depression also have prominent symptoms of anxiety. Anxiety refers to excessive worry that is hard to control (apprehensive expectation). A person with anxiety feels restless, keyed up or on edge. The person may also tire easily; feel his or her mind going blank; feel irritable; or have tense muscles, trouble concentrating and sleep problems. The combination of depressive and anxiety symptoms can severely impair a person's ability to function at work, at school and in relationships.

If you have symptoms of both depression and anxiety, a thorough assessment should determine which of the two is the primary problem. The diagnosis will influence what kind of treatment is suggested. If it is difficult to tell which is the primary disorder, a diagnosis of mixed anxiety-depressive disorder will be made, and treatment will be prescribed accordingly.

Many of the medications used to treat depression, such as citalopram (Celexa), escitalopram (Cipralex), sertraline (Zoloft), venlafaxine (Effexor), duloxetine (Cymbalta) and desvenlafaxine (Pristiq) also treat anxiety. A person might also benefit from an anti-anxiety medication or **anxiolytic** such as lorazepam (Ativan). Cognitive-behavioural therapy, a short-term talk therapy described in the next chapter, has been very effective in treating both depression and anxiety. Other helpful treatments include relaxation therapy, and stress management techniques.

WHY DO PEOPLE WITH DEPRESSION OFTEN AVOID OTHER PEOPLE?

Even though loneliness and a lack of social supports can contribute to and maintain depression, some people with depression want to be left alone. The symptoms of depression make socializing and interacting with friends and family very difficult and even stressful. Additionally, people who are depressed often feel guilty about it, and assume that their presence cannot be tolerated by others. Unfortunately, the resulting social isolation simply reinforces their depression. Part of recovery involves encouraging people with depression to gradually reintroduce themselves to social situations and structured group activities.

SHOULD PEOPLE WITH DEPRESSION FORCE THEMSELVES TO CONTINUE WITH ROUTINES AND ACTIVITIES?

If you are mildly depressed, but still able to carry on with some or all of your regular activities, you should push yourself to do so. If there is no routine to your day, you may dwell on problems and make your depression worse. If you are severely depressed and find it physically and emotionally impossible to carry out your normal activities, you should treat your depression the same way you would treat a severe physical illness. Adjust your expectations of yourself, set small goals for each day, and rest when your body needs it.

CAN I RETURN TO NORMAL AFTER BEING DEPRESSED?

Most people are able to return to their previous level of functioning. For people who have had severe depressive episodes, or several depressive episodes, recovery can be a much slower process. Setting small, achievable goals, which may be far lower than those you would have set when you were well, will be an important first step in recovery. Professional support can help you develop a graduated plan for returning to work, school or volunteer activities.

HAVING HAD ONE DEPRESSIVE EPISODE, WILL I BE AT RISK OF MORE PERIODS OF CLINICAL DEPRESSION?

Research suggests that people who have had one episode of depression have a 50 per cent chance of experiencing another episode at some point in their lives. After two depressive episodes there is an 80 per cent chance of relapse. *While these numbers may frighten you, the best protection against relapse is the understanding that depression is an illness that must be managed over your lifetime, even during periods of health.* This is why it is so important for people with depression, and their partners and families, to have information about the disorder and strategies for relapse prevention.

Common questions about acute episodes

WHAT SHOULD I DO IF I FEEL SUICIDAL OR FEEL LIKE HARMING OTHER PEOPLE?

If you feel so depressed that you wish you were dead or you are thinking of ways to kill yourself or others, tell your doctor immediately. If you do not have a doctor, call your local distress centre or go for help to the emergency department of the nearest general or psychiatric hospital. It is important that you have someone with whom you can talk and who has a more objective point of view. Suicidal thinking is the result of your depression "talking," and negatively influencing how you see yourself and the world around you.

WILL I BE KEPT IN HOSPITAL AGAINST MY WILL IF I AM SUICIDAL?

Most people who are suicidal recognize that they need treatment and find that hospitalization is a way to stay safe while their mood stabilizes. However, in most jurisdictions, if you do not recognize that you need hospitalization, or once admitted you want to leave in order to harm yourself or others, you can be legally certified by a doctor and prevented from leaving until your safety can be ensured. This certification will last only as long as is thought necessary. In most hospitals, patients may consult a rights advisor or have access to an appeal process to challenge an involuntary hospitalization.

WILL I BE COMPLETELY WELL WHEN I LEAVE THE HOSPITAL?

Probably not. Most patients are kept in hospital only in order to get their acute symptoms, such as suicidal thinking, under control and managed by medication. Then plans are made for ongoing follow-up from mental health care providers in the community. Because the process of recovery is slow, and it is important for people to resume normal routines in their homes, hospital stays are kept as brief as possible. In addition, some people with depression may feel too upset by the institutional setting, being around other ill people, and being away from family and friends to benefit from an extended hospital stay.

3 Treatments for depression

People with depression are often seen first by their family doctor or general practitioner. In milder cases, family doctors can assess and treat you as an outpatient with medication, counselling or both. They may refer you to other community resources (e.g., counselling services, drop-in centres).

If your depressive symptoms are more severe, a family doctor may refer you to a psychiatrist, who can treat you as an outpatient or, if necessary, admit you to hospital. In some settings, hospital psychiatrists are consultants to your family doctor and may see you only once or for a few visits to recommend the best treatment options.

In deciding the best plan for treatment, the doctor will consider the severity of your illness, events that may have triggered its onset, and, if applicable, previous treatments you have undergone.

Treatments for depression include psychosocial treatments (e.g., psychotherapy, psychoeducation) and biological treatments (e.g., medications, brain intervention therapies). These treatments may be used individually or in combination. It is very helpful for a person's partner or family to learn about the disorder, either through reading materials, attending a family support and education group or talking with a mental health care provider.

Psychosocial treatments

PSYCHOTHERAPY

Psychotherapy is often used along with medication to treat depression. Psychotherapy is a general term used to describe a form of treatment that is based on "talking work" done with a therapist. The aim is to relieve distress by discussing and expressing feelings, to help change attitudes, behaviour and habits that may be unhelpful, and to promote more constructive and adaptive ways of coping.

Successful psychotherapy depends on a supportive, comfortable relationship with a trusted therapist. Psychiatrists, social workers, psychologists and other mental health providers are trained in various models of psychotherapy, and work in hospitals, clinics and private practice.

There are many different treatment models of psychotherapy for individuals. **Short-term models** usually last up to 16 weeks. These therapies include **interpersonal therapy** (IPT), cognitive-behavioural therapy (CBT) and mindfulness-based cognitive therapy (MBCT). They are structured and focus on current, rather than childhood, issues, and the therapist takes an active role in guiding the discussions. Research has found these therapies to be very effective in treating depression.

In IPT, people examine their depression in the context of relationships that may be contributing to their mood difficulties (for example, changes in relationship roles, such as becoming a parent or ongoing conflict in an important relationship).

CBT helps people examine how they interpret events around them, and how negative thoughts contribute to and maintain a depressed mood.

MBCT is a recent development that has grown out of research into the benefits of *mindfulness*. Mindfulness and MBCT use meditation techniques to help people let go of focusing on their negative thoughts. MBCT is used specifically to help prevent relapse for people who have experienced multiple episodes of depression.

Long-term therapy is less structured, and can last for a year or more. The person has the opportunity to talk about a variety of concerns related to both past and present-day issues. In general, the therapist helps the client to relate how current events trigger issues from childhood, which may now be impairing the person's performance in relationships, at work or at school. In this model, the therapist is less directive and gives minimal advice, guiding the client instead toward his or her own answers.

Therapy can also be provided in a group context. Meeting with eight to 12 other people who are struggling with similar issues can help reduce a person's sense of isolation. The kind of support, understanding and feedback found in group therapy may not be available within a person's own natural social network. Groups are generally led by one or two mental health care providers who guide the group process and offer structure and direction where needed. Some groups may be process oriented; that is, they focus on the issues the group members raise each week, rather than having a set agenda. Other groups may be quite structured, such as groups that follow cognitive-behavioural therapy. In these groups, the members work through a step-by-step process, often guided by a manual that helps them to focus on dealing with attitudes and behaviours that contribute to and help maintain depression. Not all structured groups, however, require the use of a manual.

Whether short- or long-term, psychotherapy can be used in combination with medication, and can help you to resolve issues that
may be contributing to your depression and affecting your overall
life situation.

How do I find a psychotherapist?

It is worth the time and effort required to find a psychotherapist
with whom you feel comfortable. Speak with your family doctor
about therapists in your area. These may include psychiatrists
(who provide both medication therapy and psychotherapy); general
practitioner psychotherapists; or private social workers, psychologists or other mental health care providers. Contact the outpatient
departments of the general and psychiatric hospitals' in your area
to find out if they offer individual or group psychotherapy. Your
local mental health association may offer a referral service. Finally,
do not overlook the network of "word-of-mouth" information available through mutual aid organizations and other people struggling
with depression.

PSYCHOEDUCATION

Psychoeducation is a process through which people learn about depression, and also have an opportunity to talk about their feelings
related to living and coping with the disorder. For example, it is
common for people learning about their depression to experience
strong feelings of fear or denial. Often, talking openly about these
feelings helps people to deal with them and better adhere to a treatment plan that makes sense to them. Psychoeducation can occur
in groups or in individual counselling with a doctor, social worker
or other mental health care provider. When psychoeducation is
offered in a group format it is usually time-limited (8 to 12 sessions) and each session focuses on a different aspect of managing

depression (for example, signs and symptoms, stress management and problem solving).

Psychoeducation also helps family members or partners understand what the affected person is going through. They learn about the symptoms of depression, its treatment, what they can do to be helpful, and the limitations to the help that they can offer. The family can meet with the treating doctor or therapist, or attend a family support and education group.

Finally, psychoeducation helps people with depression and their families to deal with their concerns about the stigma of mental illness. Although public education in recent years has raised awareness, there are still many people who do not understand depression as a disorder, and feel uncomfortable when it is discussed. It is important that people with depression, along with their families, have a safe place to discuss this issue and decide what information they wish to share outside of the family.

FAMILY AND COUPLE THERAPY

Depression can have a profound impact, both on the people with the disorder and on their families. During an acute episode, partners and family members may have to assume the roles and responsibilities of the ill person. As a person recovers, his or her partner and family may struggle to re-establish old routines. Sometimes, their feelings about what has happened, and fears about the future, make it difficult for things to "get back to normal." This may lead to marital or family conflict. Also, pre-existing family or marital stressors may have contributed to the onset of the depressive episode. In these situations, couple or family counselling can be very helpful.

PEER SUPPORT GROUPS

An important part of treatment and recovery, both for people with depression and for their families, is the chance to meet informally with other people who understand their issues and challenges. Peer-support groups, run by clients of the mental health system and their families, are usually located in major cities and may have chapters in smaller centres; they often have newsletters or websites that can reach people who live in isolated communities. Attending these groups can reduce a person's sense of isolation, and provides opportunities to learn from other group members' experiences. For many people, volunteering in these organizations and sharing the wisdom they have gained by living with depression can also be an empowering experience. See the Resources section on page 58 for more information. Peer-support groups can also be found through your local mental health association, your community mental health services, or your family doctor. Although these groups are often called *self-help*, peer support actually offers a type of help called *mutual aid*.

Biological treatments

MEDICATIONS

Antidepressant medications can relieve and resolve the symptoms of depression. With early intervention, medication can prevent people from developing a severe depressive episode, and preserve their current coping skills. Medication also allows people to make better use of talking therapies than is possible when they are acutely withdrawn and depressed. With more severe depressions, medication offers symptom relief and restores patients' moods to a more neutral level, enabling them to return to regular routines and activities.

Antidepressants are thought to work primarily by affecting the concentration of chemicals called **neurotransmitters** in the brain. Key neurotransmitters that are affected include serotonin, norepinephrine and dopamine.

Antidepressant medications can take up to several weeks to be fully effective. Early signs that the medication is working include improved sleep, appetite and energy. Improvement in mood usually comes later. To get the best effect from an antidepressant, a doctor will gradually increase the dosage to the highest level at which it will have a therapeutic effect. In addition, the doctor may boost the effect of an antidepressant by adding another medication (e.g., the drug lithium may be chosen to augment the primary antidepressant). Once the medication has relieved the symptoms of depression, it is often recommended that patients continue to take it for up to one year, or more, in order to avoid relapse. When patients have been well for a period of time, they may be gradually tapered off the antidepressant under the supervision of a community health care provider.

Common worries about antidepressants include the fear of becoming addicted to the medication. Antidepressants are not addictive and serve an important role in the treatment of depression. In addition, many people hesitate to take medications because they view reliance on them as a sign of weakness. This suggests that they view depression as a weakness in character, rather than a legitimate medical disorder. But depression *is* an illness that, without treatment, can worsen significantly and even become life-threatening. Other common questions about antidepressants are answered in the pamphlet *Understanding Psychiatric Medications: Antidepressants*, available from the Centre for Addiction and Mental Health. The pamphlet includes questions about starting and stopping antidepressants; interactions with alcohol, caffeine or other drugs; driving safety; sexuality and pregnancy; and age. An online version is available at www.camh.ca.

Because depression is a complex disorder, many psychiatrists now specialize in the biology of depression and medication treatments. It is important to have a prescribing doctor with whom you feel comfortable asking questions about medications, their effectiveness and their side-effects.

Side-effects vary depending on the type of antidepressant you are taking. Some people experience no side-effects. Others may find the side-effects distressing. In most cases, side-effects lessen as treatment continues. Treatment is usually started at a low dose, to minimize side-effects, and then slowly increased until the ideal dose is found. The ideal dose is one that provides the greatest benefit with minimum side-effects. If side-effects are not mild and tolerable, it is best to continue taking your medication as prescribed and let your doctor know as soon as possible.

Types of antidepressants

The information in this section is summarized from the CAMH pamphlet series *Understanding Psychiatric Medications*. The pamphlets are designed to help people better understand and make choices about psychiatric drugs. They discuss what the drugs are used for, the different types and names of drugs, their effects and their place in the treatment of mental health problems. Online versions are available at www.camh.ca.

There are several classes of antidepressants; within each class there are many individual medications. While all antidepressants work well overall, no drug or type of drug works equally well for everyone who takes it. Some people may be advised to try another type of antidepressant or to use a combination of antidepressants to seek relief from their distress.

The different types of antidepressants are listed below in the order in which they are most commonly prescribed.

SELECTIVE SEROTONIN REUPTAKE INHIBITORS (SSRIs)

This group of medications includes fluoxetine (Prozac), paroxetine (Paxil), fluvoxamine (Luvox), citalopram (Celexa), escitalopram (Cipralex) and sertraline (Zoloft). SSRIs are usually the first choice for treatment of depression and anxiety problems. These medications are known to have milder side-effects than some other antidepressants. Buspirone (Buspar) is similar to SSRIs and has been found to help with anxiety but not depression.

SEROTONIN AND NOREPINEPHRINE REUPTAKE INHIBITORS (SNRIs)

This class of medications includes venlafaxine (Effexor), duloxetine (Cymbalta) and desvenlafaxine (Pristiq). These drugs are used to treat depression, anxiety problems and chronic pain.

NOREPINEPHRINE AND DOPAMINE REUPTAKE INHIBITORS (NDRIs)

The medication available in this class is bupropion (Wellbutrin, Zyban). When used to treat depression, it is often given for its energizing effects, in combination with other antidepressants. It is also used to treat attention-deficit/hyperactivity disorder and as a smoking cessation aid.

NORADRENERGIC AND SPECIFIC SEROTONERGIC ANTIDEPRESSANTS (NASSAs)

Mirtazapine (Remeron), the medication available in this class, is the most sedating antidepressant, making it a good choice for people who have insomnia or who are very anxious. This medication also helps to stimulate appetite.

CYCLICS

This older group includes amitriptyline (Elavil), maprotiline (Ludiomil), imipramine (Tofranil), desipramine (Norpramin), nortriptyline (Novo-Nortriptyline) and clomipramine (Anafranil).

Because these drugs tend to have more side-effects than the newer drugs, they are not often a first choice for treatment. However, when other drugs do not provide relief from severe depression, these drugs may help.

MONOAMINE OXIDASE INHIBITORS (MAOIs)

MAOIs, such as phenelzine (Nardil) and tranylcypromine (Parnate), were the first class of antidepressants. MAOIs are effective, but they are not often used because people who take them must follow a special diet.

A newer MAOI, moclobemide (Manerix), can be used without dietary restrictions; however, it may not be as effective as other MAOIs.

LIGHT THERAPY FOR SEASONAL AFFECTIVE DISORDER

Light therapy—spending half an hour every day under a specially designed light box—can provide relief for 65 per cent of people diagnosed with seasonal affective disorder (SAD). It usually takes between one and three weeks for patients to respond to the therapy. Light therapy is thought to correct the disturbance of circadian rhythms during the fall and winter months.

BRAIN INTERVENTION THERAPIES

This group of treatments (also known as neurostimulation) involves stimulating regions of the brain with either an electric current or a magnetic field.

Electroconvulsive therapy

Electroconvulsive therapy (ECT), also referred to as "shock therapy," is a long-standing, effective and widely misunderstood treatment for acute depression. It has been both condemned and promoted in the mental health field and the media. In its early days, ECT was a cruder procedure that resulted in short- and longer-term memory loss. For most of these patients, however, memory problems resolved after six months.

Today, ECT remains the most effective treatment for major depression. However, it is usually seen as a last resort because of people's fears and misconceptions. Doctors usually treat patients with less intrusive methods, such as medication, before moving on to ECT if necessary.

ECT does not resemble the shock therapy portrayed in films such as *One Flew over the Cuckoo's Nest.* Now patients are given muscle relaxants and a general anesthetic before a mild electrical current is administered to one or both sides of the brain. There is minimal visible movement in the patient during the procedure.

It is not clear how ECT works, but after about five treatments, usually given every other day, most patients' moods begin to improve. A course of eight to 18 treatments may be offered, depending on the patient's response. Many patients with severe depression, who have been disappointed by the failure of medications to relieve their symptoms, find ECT "kickstarts" them out of an acute depressive state. The improvements can then be maintained with medications, occasional ECT treatments and psychotherapy or rehabilitative therapy.

SIDE-EFFECTS

Patients may have a headache or jaw pain on awakening after ECT, usually requiring only a mild painkiller such as acetaminophen (Tylenol). Some loss of recent memory or problems with concentration usually occur during treatment (e.g., patients may not recall what they had for supper the night before the treatment), but these symptoms improve quickly after the course of ECT is finished, over a few weeks. Some patients report mild memory problems persisting much longer after ECT treatment has been completed.

Transcranial magnetic stimulation and magnetic seizure therapy

Transcranial magnetic stimulation (TMS) involves a series of short magnetic pulses directed to the brain to stimulate nerve cells. TMS is being investigated as an alternative treatment to ECT, but its effectiveness is not yet proven. Unlike ECT, the treatment is carried out without the need for an anesthetic or muscle relaxant. **Magnetic seizure therapy** (MST) involves the production of a seizure by a large dose magnetic stimulation directed to the brain. MST was developed as an alternative to ECT in order to find a beneficial treatment for depression with minimal cognitive side-effects. The benefits of MST are currently being tested.

COMPLEMENTARY AND ALTERNATIVE THERAPIES

Some people with depression seek non-conventional treatments, often as an adjunct to complement conventional treatments rather than as an alternative. Examples of complementary treatments include herbal medicines, acupuncture, homeopathy, naturopathy, meditation, yoga and Ayurveda. A number of nutritional supplements and vitamins are also available.

Many of these treatments have not been thoroughly tested. St. John's wort has been shown to have some antidepressant effect for mild to moderate depression.

If you are interested in herbal remedies, it is important to talk to your doctor. It is helpful to have a doctor who is knowledgeable about complementary and alternative therapies, because they can interact with other medications you may be taking.

Some people find that practices such as yoga, tai chi and meditation can aid with the control of anxiety and depression.

Physical activity

Physical activity or exercise has been shown to have antidepressant effect. Regular physical activity—even just walking for 30 minutes a day—has profound effects for physical and mental health. Exercise has also been shown to increase the size of the hippocampus, a part of the brain concerned with memory.

4 Recovery and relapse prevention

The process of recovery

People define recovery from depression in their own, individual ways. Some people think of it as a process, while others think of it as a goal or an end result. Whatever your personal approach, it is helpful to remember that you are a person first and foremost. A mental health label does not define you: you are not "depression," you are an individual. People recovering from mild depression usually resume their regular routines and responsibilities quite easily. Recovery from a more serious and lengthy depression can be a longer-term and slower process. A long period of illness can lower a person's self-confidence, making him or her feel insecure and vulnerable in situations that used to be familiar and comfortable. Depression can cause people to become quite dependent on those around them. People are often surprised at how frightened they are at the prospect of being independent and resuming their responsibilities.

It is important to recognize that these reactions are a normal part of the recovery phase of depression. *Give yourself permission to adjust your expectations; you are recovering from a serious illness.* Just as you would increase activities gradually if you were recovering from a broken leg, a gradual increase in activities following a depressive episode will allow you to slowly take on responsibilities and build your self-confidence. Some people rush into a full schedule of activities in order to prove to themselves and others that they are fully recovered. This "flight into health" leaves them feeling overwhelmed and exhausted. If you have high expectations of yourself, or you like things to be perfect, you are likely to feel dissatisfied at your rate of recovery and feel hopeless and demoralized that things are not working out exactly right.

Remember that recovery is a process, not a single event. At first, you should ease yourself into familiar activities and have modest expectations. Predict that when you return to activities such as socializing and going to school or work, you will probably feel anxious. Allow yourself to make mistakes. A social worker, occupational therapist or nurse can help you plan a strategy for recovery that might include volunteer activities, leisure interests, school courses, and part-time or eventually full-time work.

Preventing relapse and promoting wellness

People who have had a major depressive episode are at risk of further episodes. *It is important to use periods of wellness as an opportunity to actively prevent relapse.* Depression, like illnesses such as diabetes, requires you to pay attention to how you are feeling, so you can catch early warnings of a possible relapse and possibly prevent a full depressive episode.

1. **Become an expert on your illness.** Read as much as you can about depression and its treatment; if there is something you do not understand, ask your mental health care providers.

2. **Monitor changes in your mood and include activities that have a positive effect on your mood.** When you are feeling better, pay attention to the variations in your moods. Don't ignore changes, such as sleep disturbances or negative or hopeless thoughts, that may suggest a potential relapse. Pay attention to activities that help to stabilize or improve how you are feeling, and incorporate these into your everyday activities. For example, if walking your dog or visiting friends is helpful, make sure these are part of your structured routines. (Also see "Recognizing and Responding to Early Warning Signs and Triggers" below.)

3. **If medication has been prescribed, continue to take it until your doctor advises you otherwise.** Often, people begin to feel better and stop taking their medication. Relapse is more likely if medication is discontinued too soon. Doctors usually recommend that medication be taken for six months to a year following a depressive episode. For some conditions, antidepressants may be recommended for several years. If you are experiencing side-effects, you may be tempted to stop taking your medication. Rather than making decisions on your own, work with your doctor around a treatment plan you can live with.

4. **Live healthily.** It makes sense to pay special attention to these areas if you are struggling with depression. Fatigue is worsened if you eat very little, or eat an unhealthy diet. Research has demonstrated that regular exercise can have a positive effect on mood.

If you are struggling with falling asleep or staying asleep, it is important for you to develop good sleep routines. Repeating these routines each night can help restore better sleep patterns.

Try to go to bed at the same time each night. Avoid stimulating activities close to bedtime; plan on paying bills, completing work or having important discussions earlier in the day. Many people find that relaxation exercises, easy reading or a warm, non-caffeinated beverage just before retiring are ways to promote a relaxed state of mind. Expect that it will take you some time to fall asleep and try not to anticipate sleep problems, as this will add to your anxiety. For some people, a sleep medication provides relief and allows them the much-needed rest they have been deprived of due to depression.

5. **Think about whether any features of your personality may lead to depressive thinking.** If you tend to view circumstances and events around you in an overly negative way, if you worry a lot, if you have trouble expressing your feelings, or if you tend to be inflexible or perfectionistic, you might benefit from psychotherapy. Through psychotherapy you can learn to address these issues and build on your strengths.

6. **You cannot avoid stress, so find strategies to better cope with stress.** Many people with depression tend to use only one coping strategy. For example, they hide their worries and avoid dealing with problems. This may work in some cases, but not in others. Where possible, try different strategies. Deal with some problems as they happen. Avoiding them allows stress to build up. Be realistic about your stress-breaking point. Work toward recognizing what aspects of relationships in your life might be unhealthy and, if possible, try to avoid situations that may trigger relapse.

7. **Avoid isolating yourself and maintain social support.** Spending too much time alone can contribute to depression and relapse, yet the feelings of depression often make people want to isolate themselves. Strong social networks and social support can serve as a buffer against depression. Try to avoid spending too

much time alone, and work toward maintaining contact with your social network.

Whom you tell about your depression is a very personal choice. While the stigma of mental illness is much less than it once was, it remains a concern for many people. As a buffer against relapse, however, it is important to have at least one person you can rely on and you can confide in. Along with family and professional support, many people with depression find that peer support groups are a valuable part of their social network.

8. **Try to develop a balanced life.** It might seem easy at first to escape from your depression by focusing entirely on one area, such as work or a hobby. Eventually, however, this coping strategy may not work, and you will need to develop other aspects of your life. It is important to keep in contact with all the facets of your life, such as school, work or volunteer activities, family and friends, and hobbies. As you recover, investing energy in several areas will help you develop a more balanced and satisfying life, which will help you to avoid relapse.

9. **Get follow-up treatment.** It is important to have a family doctor and, if necessary, a psychiatrist who can follow up with you regularly. Depending on your needs, you may also benefit from individual, group or family therapy, or a support group, to help you deal with the impact that depression has had on your life. If you start to feel depressed again, contact your doctor immediately. Help may come in the form of a visiting nurse, an occupational therapist, or a social worker who can provide extra support when necessary. Early intervention may help to prevent, or minimize the severity of, another depressive episode.

10. **Finally, be aware that it is common, after recovery, to silently worry about relapse.** Think about establishing a crisis plan with

your family, your partner or a friend, just in case you begin to feel unwell again. This plan will include knowing who will take care of things should you need to be hospitalized: who will notify your doctor and take you to appointments, notify your school or workplace, look after your children, and ensure that your rent or mortgage and bills are paid. You may feel less anxious about the future if you know that a backup plan exists.

Recognizing and responding to early warning signs and triggers

When you return to school, work, or home and community involvement, it is important to learn to recognize and respond to early warning signs such as subtle changes in your mood. Focusing on ways to concentrate better and to work more efficiently may also help. You may also benefit from decreasing some of the external stresses in your environment.

Typical signs of starting to feel depressed are:

• trouble concentrating and focusing or completing tasks
• lower energy level and confidence
• sensitivity about the comments of others
• increased worry
• doubting the worth of daily involvement in activities
• trouble making fairly simple decisions
• changes in sleep and appetite.

It is also important to learn to identify your personal triggers, and make plans to cope effectively when they arise. Triggers are external events or circumstances that can precede mood changes. Some examples are:

- anniversary dates
- financial problems
- conflict with an important person
- being in an abusive situation
- physical illness, such as flu.

When you are depressed or are experiencing triggers, you may find it helps to:

- recognize some of the symptoms, and speak to your doctor to see if your medications need to be adjusted or if other treatments may be needed
- seek out family members, friends or co-workers to support you and realistically assess your impressions
- focus on completing simpler, concrete tasks, and delay the harder and more challenging tasks if possible
- delay making any important decisions
- limit time in more public and/or socially demanding activities
- structure your day to include more activities that you find rewarding
- set goals to address these mood changes; for example, make sure you are involved in enjoyable activities with people who support you.

5 Help for partners and families

What happens when someone you love has depression?

When a family member has a serious illness, it affects your entire family. This is true of a physical illness, such as diabetes, or a mental illness, such as depression. When your relative or partner has a mental illness, you must cope with extra stressors, such as stigma. Fearing prejudice, your family may try to deal with mental illness alone. Furthermore, depression will affect your relative's mood and behaviour. At times, your family member's mood disorder can make them less able to manage the illness, and the person may become less able to work with you to solve problems. This may include changes in how the person can attend to their usual roles and responsibilities.

As a family member, you will likely find the illness very distressing. If your family member only has mild depression, you may be able to get through it without too much trouble. But if your relative's depression is severe, you will likely find it hard to handle.

Seeing a loved one struggle with depression can make people feel sad, concerned, frightened, helpless and anxious. You may experience guilt, anger and frustration. All depressive episodes are upsetting, but the first one will probably be especially confusing. You may not understand what is happening and why the person is not getting better on his or her own. Without information about depression, you might assume that your relative is lazy, or you may give well-meaning advice and become frustrated and annoyed when he or she does not act on it. If your relative talks about suicide, you will understandably live with a great deal of worry.

How to relate to a person with depression

Family members often do not know how to talk to a person who is depressed. They may be afraid to ask too many questions and inadvertently upset their loved one. At the same time, they do not want the ill person to feel that they are not interested or are avoiding him or her.

Try to be as supportive, understanding and patient as possible. Just recognizing that depression is an illness can help your relative to feel less guilty about his or her impaired functioning.

Tips for communication

1. Speak in a **calm, quiet voice.**

2. **Focus on one subject** at a time. Your relative or friend may have trouble concentrating.

3. If the person is quiet and withdrawn, break the ice with **neutral, non-threatening statements**, such as "It seems a bit warm in here."

4. **Be patient and wait.** It may take a while for your loved one to respond.

5. **Your ability to listen is a valuable resource to your relative.** Depression causes people to talk a lot about how bad they feel, yet they may not be ready to discuss solutions to their problems. Listening and letting the person know, in a neutral manner, that you have heard what he or she has said, is valuable and supportive. You do not have to offer immediate solutions.

6. **If the person is irritable, you probably need to slow down, adjust your expectations and use a very neutral approach.** Neutral comments about the weather, what you are making for dinner or other routine subjects are the safest way to develop a dialogue. Listen for opportunities to acknowledge or add to your relative's responses. At these times, conversations about important decisions or issues are unlikely to be productive. You may need to plan to discuss important issues at a later date.

7. **Avoid quizzing people about what made them feel depressed. Do not blame them for the way they feel, or tell them to snap out of it.** People who are moderately depressed may be able to hear your helpful suggestions, but be unable to act on your advice. Quizzing or blaming them will only reinforce their guilt, loneliness and isolation. Often, people with depression cannot identify what made them depressed or what will be helpful.

8. **Pace yourself.** If your relative is severely or more chronically depressed, it is normal for you to find his or her company very draining. Brief, frequent contacts are often the best way to re-

late to someone with severe depression. If your relative is hospitalized, family members might take turns visiting.

Getting treatment for your family member

FOLLOWING THROUGH WITH TREATMENT

While many people are open to seeking treatment for depression, others are reluctant to admit their difficulties. Some people with depression worry that admitting to their depressed feelings is a sign of weakness, or that they will be stigmatized for having psychiatric problems. Others try to cope on their own and do not realize until they are acutely depressed that they have a disorder that can be treated.

If you are worried about a loved one who appears depressed, but is not currently receiving treatment, just letting him or her know that help exists may be enough to get the person to seek treatment. For some people, it is a long and bumpy road to accepting that they have a disorder that must be managed over their lifespan. Some people must experience several depressive episodes before they consistently accept help from doctors and therapists. As a family member, it can be very difficult to watch this process without trying repeatedly to convince the person to "take your medication" or "go and talk to your doctor." Repeated attempts to convince and cajole can lead to heated arguments and power struggles. If you are very close to the person with depression, and yet you feel that he or she may not be open to your observation that something is wrong, it may be more effective to have another trusted person approach your relative.

SUICIDAL THOUGHTS

People who are depressed to the point of thinking about suicide may refuse treatment because they feel so hopeless and worthless. In this case, you or another trusted person should insist that the person see his or her doctor or go to the emergency department of a local hospital. Many people will agree to go to hospital. If the person refuses, there are a number of options the family can take. For example, you can go to a justice of the peace to get an order allowing police to take the person to hospital for an assessment. If there is an immediate risk of suicide, you should call 911.

Involving the police is a painful and difficult decision, though it is sometimes necessary in order to get an ill person to the hospital. Family members often feel overwhelmingly guilty about this decision, even when it is necessary to protect the person's life. It is important to remember that when people threaten suicide, they are usually making a plea for help, which should be taken seriously. Suicidal thinking is usually a temporary emotional state during which a person needs to be in a place of safety.

YOUR FAMILY MEMBER IN HOSPITAL

Once in hospital, if your relative is quite ill and impaired, it is sometimes better for both the patient and the family if visits are frequent but short. People who are acutely ill do not benefit from long conversations in which they can become overwhelmed as they ruminate, or repeatedly focus on their feelings of hopelessness and negativity. Frequent, brief contacts allow you to stay in touch with your relative, and reassure him or her that you remain supportive.

For some people, being in hospital is very challenging because their movements may be restricted to ensure safety They may wish to leave the hospital before the professional staff feel their mood and behaviour are stabilized. For family members, this is particularly difficult as they can foresee the problems at home if the person becomes acutely ill again and requires hospitalization. Some patients will respond to the concerns of friends and family and agree to stay longer in hospital. This is more easily accomplished if there are clear goals to be achieved during the admission. For example, it might be helpful to concretely state that the person must be stabilized on medication and connected with a day program or community therapist before discharge.

Most jurisdictions in North America have mental health legislation that permits involuntary hospitalization of people only if they threaten to harm themselves or other people, or cannot care for themselves. Many ill people who would benefit from hospitalization do not meet these criteria and therefore may leave the hospital against medical advice.

In these situations, try to negotiate with your relative when it might be best to leave the hospital. What must be accomplished during the admission for you to feel it is safe for the person to return home? Could these issues be discussed in a **discharge planning meeting** with your relative, the doctor and any other care providers who work with him or her?

Sometimes, you can help your relative slow down saying that you need this meeting to take place before consenting to his or her returning home. Families often feel guilty at insisting on these conditions, because they worry that their loved one will feel rejected. However, the result of premature discharge and poor discharge planning is frequently a relapse in the illness and a more complicated situation.

Care for partners and families

When someone has a serious illness, it is natural for family members to feel worried and stressed. In an effort to spend time comforting or helping their loved one, family members may give up their own activities. Unsure of how others may respond to their ill partner or relative, they may also avoid having friends visit their home. Over time, they may become isolated from their own network of friends, or find that most of their normal routines and activities have been replaced by the demands of caring for their loved one. Often, they are well into this situation before they realize how emotionally and physically drained they have become. This stress can lead to sleep disturbances, exhaustion or chronic irritability.

It is important to recognize these signs of stress in yourself and look after your own physical and mental health. Recognizing your own limitations and making time for yourself are key elements in "self-care." Ensure that you have a good support system of reliable friends and relatives. Think about whom you want to share the details of the situation with. Mental illness is a difficult thing for some people to make sense of, so it is understandable if you want to be selective and choose only people who you know will be supportive.

Families and partners need to get as much information as possible about depression. Knowledge and understanding will improve your ability to help and support your loved one, deal with your own feelings, and explain the situation to extended family, friends and colleagues. Information is available from the treating doctor, social worker or other mental health care providers. In addition to this publication, there are many books written for people with depression and their families. They are usually available through public libraries.

Consider getting professional support for yourself, and joining a peer-support group or family support program, which may be offered at a local hospital or community mental health clinic. Keep up your interests outside the family and apart from your ill relative. Acknowledge and accept that sometimes you will have negative feelings about the situation. These feelings are normal and should not be a source of guilt.

How you can support recovery

Once your relative is stabilized, you will likely observe the person make slow but steady improvement. Over time, he or she may want to discontinue medication, because of the side-effects, or psychotherapy, because of the time commitment involved. Your support in encouraging your loved one to remain in treatment can be very important. Stopping medication too soon can contribute to relapse, and reducing or stopping medication should be monitored by a doctor. Psychotherapy works best if the client and the therapist mutually agree that the person's emotional work is complete, or the agreed number of sessions has been reached.

Family members, partners and friends are important figures in a person's support network. "Just being there" and keeping up an interest in the person is an important contribution to the recovery process. Once recovered from depression, people often acknowledge how much they appreciated the presence and tolerance of their families and friends.

The recovering person will enter a transitional phase where he or she gradually resumes previous responsibilities. Your relative might benefit from help with making decisions about first steps. Be aware though that giving your opinion before you are asked may be experienced as controlling. Try to do things *with* the person, rather than *for* the person. Encourage the person to be as active as possible. Recognize that your relative is an independent adult, who may choose activities or behaviours that you disagree with. Avoid saying that the person has made a wrong choice because he or she is ill; this can be hurtful and can complicate your relationship.

As your loved one's health improves, treat him or her increasingly as a well person, including the person in family activities, discussions and responsibilities around the house. Avoid addressing and resolving problems through loud arguments and debates, or openly expressing hostility and anger. While this kind of conflict is common in some families, research suggests that it puts people recovering from depression at greater risk of relapse. Be sensitive to the needs of your recovering relative, and understand that he or she might not be able to manage the highly charged emotions associated with conflict and arguments. Consider other ways of dealing with family disputes, such as family counselling.

Being ready for a relapse or crisis

People with depression and their families often avoid talking about acute crises because these events are uncomfortable to acknowledge and awkward to discuss. However, the best way to handle a crisis is to know what to do before it happens. It is important to focus on maintaining wellness, but some planning for a possible crisis can create a sense of security for the ill person and the family.

When your family member is well, discuss what you will do if he or she should become ill or suicidal again. Could you visit your relative's doctor together to discuss his or her condition and the possibility of a crisis? If your relative became ill, would you have permission in advance to contact his or her doctor? Would you have consent to take the person to the hospital, and which hospital is preferred? If your loved one were acutely ill, would you be allowed to make decisions? Could you put the conditions of an agreement in writing to ensure that these instructions were followed?

A prearranged crisis plan and a good working relationship with your relative's doctor and other care providers can help to contain an emergency situation.

6 Explaining depression to children

Explaining depression or other mental illness to children can be awkward and difficult. To protect their children, the parent with depression and the well parent (if present) may choose to say nothing and try to continue with family routines as if nothing were wrong. While this may provide a short-term solution, over the long term it can leave children confused and worried about the changes in behaviour that they have inevitably noticed.

Children are sensitive and intuitive, and quickly notice when someone in the family has changed. If the atmosphere in the family suggests that the subject should not be discussed, children will draw their own, often incorrect, conclusions. Young children, especially those of pre-school or elementary school age, often see the world as revolving around themselves. If something negative or difficult happens, they assume they did something to cause it. For example, if a child disobeys a parent and gets into trouble, and the next morning the parent is depressed, the child may assume that he or she caused the parent's depression.

To explain mental illness and depression to children, you provide them with as much information as they are mature enough to understand. Toddlers and pre-school children are able to understand simple, short sentences, without much technical information. School-age children can process more information, but may be overwhelmed by details about medications and therapies. Teenagers are generally able to manage most information, and often need to talk about their impressions and feelings. They may have questions about how open they should be about the situation, and concerns about the stigma of mental illness. Sharing information with them provides an opening for further discussion.

It is helpful to cover three main areas:

1. **The parent or other family member behaves this way because he or she is sick.** It is important to tell children that the family member is ill with a sickness called depression. Depression makes people sad, sometimes for no reason. They might cry a lot, sleep all day and have trouble eating or talking to people. Sometimes depression takes a long time to get better, and our efforts to cheer the person up do not work.

2. **Reassure the child that he or she did not make the parent or family member sad and depressed.** Children need to be reassured that they did not cause their loved one to be unhappy through something they did or did not do. This is a frequent assumption that children will feel guilty about. Depression needs to be explained as an illness, just like having chicken pox or a bad cold.

3. **Reassure the child that the adults in the family and other people, such as doctors, are trying to help the person who is depressed. Looking after the person is an adult responsibility, and not something the child should worry about.** Children need the well parent, or other trusted adults, to serve as a buffer against the effects of a parent's depression. They may find it very helpful to talk about their feelings with someone who

empathizes with how hard it is to see their mother, father or other relative suffering. Many children are frightened by the changes in their parent. They miss the time previously spent with this parent. Participation in activities outside the home is helpful because it exposes children to other healthy relationships. As the ill parent recovers, gradually resuming family activities can help restore the relationship between the children and the ill parent.

Both the ill and the well parent should talk with the children about explaining the illness to people outside the family. Support from friends is important for everyone; however, depression can be difficult to explain, and some families are concerned about the stigma attached to mental illness. The level of openness you and your children are comfortable with is a very individual choice.

Some parents experiencing depression find that their symptoms of irritability, impatience and disorganization make it difficult to tolerate the boisterous activities and noise that are part of children's everyday play and routines. It may be necessary to take special measures to protect against events that could trigger irritability in the ill parent and cause him or her to be abrupt with the children. You may need to plan time for the children to play outside the home, or arrange for the ill parent to rest for part of the day in a quiet area of the house.

Once recovered, it is helpful for the parent who was ill to explain his or her behaviour to the children. The recovered parent may need to plan some special times with the children, to re-establish the relationship and to reassure the children that he or she is again available and interested in them.

More information on talking to children about depression is available in the pamphlet *When a Parent Is Depressed . . . What Kids Want to Know,* available from the Centre for Addiction and Mental Health. An online version is available at www.camh.ca. The CAMH children's book *Can I Catch It Like a Cold? Coping with a Parent's Depression* may also be helpful resource.

Glossary

Antidepressants: Medicines used to reduce the symptoms of depression. Antidepressants may also be used to treat other mental health problems, such as panic disorder and obsessive-compulsive disorder.

Antipsychotics: Medications that were developed to reduce psychotic symptoms. These medications are now also used to treat other mental health problems such as bipolar disorder, obsessive-compulsive disorder, severe anxiety and depression.

Anxiety: An emotional state characterized by excessive worry, apprehension or fear of impending actual or imagined danger, vulnerability or uncertainty. In a more acute form it can include intense fear and discomfort, with symptoms such as a pounding heart, sweating, shortness of breath, nausea, dizziness and fear of losing control.

Anxiolytics: Anti-anxiety medicines, such as benzodiazepines.

Atypical depression: A type of major depression in which the person has "mood reactivity," meaning he or she can be cheered up by positive events, and has at least two of the following: increased appetite or weight gain; increased sleep; leaden paralysis; easily feels rejected.

Bipolar disorder: Formerly known as manic depression; a disorder characterized by mood swings, which includes the occurrence of one or more manic or hypomanic episodes and usually one or more major depressive episodes.

Cognitive-behavioural therapy (CBT): A time-limited psychotherapy that focuses on how thoughts influence mood and how some thought patterns contribute to depression.

Delusion: A false, fixed belief not shared by your culture, such as believing that your thoughts are being controlled by forces outside you. There are various types of delusions, such as paranoid (with feelings of suspicion) and grandiose (with feelings of excessive self-importance).

Dysthymic disorder: A type of mood disorder whose main characteristic is a chronically depressed mood that lasts for most of the day, for the majority of the time during a two-year period.

Electroconvulsive therapy (ECT): A treatment procedure for severe depression that involves passing a controlled electric current between two metal discs applied on the surface of the scalp.

Hallucination: A false sensory experience, such as seeing, hearing, tasting, smelling or feeling something that does not really exist.

Hypomania: A state characterized by a high mood and overactivity, but not as extreme as mania.

Interpersonal psychotherapy (IPT): A time-limited psychotherapy that focuses on the aspects of relationships to others, which are linked to the depressive episode.

Magnetic seizure therapy (MST): A treatment for severe depression that involves stimulating the brain with magnetism to induce a seizure.

Major depressive disorder: Also known as unipolar depression; involves one or more major depressive episodes. These include symptoms such as depressed mood, loss of interest or pleasure, significant changes in weight or sleep, loss of energy, diminished capacity to think or concentrate, feelings of worthlessness or excessive guilt, and recurrent thoughts of death or suicide.

Mania: A state characterized by an unusually high mood, irritability, overactivity, excessive talkativeness, racing thoughts, inflated ideas of self, lack of insight, poor judgment, impulsiveness and financial extravagance.

Mood disorders: Disorders that have a disturbance in mood (typically depression or mania) as the predominant feature. The two main categories are unipolar depression and bipolar disorder.

Mood stabilizers: Medicines usually used to treat mania, bipolar disorder and sometimes depression.

Neurotransmitters: Chemicals that carry signals between neurons (nerve cells) in the brain. Neurotransmitters include norepinephrine, serotonin and dopamine.

Personality disorder: An enduring pattern of thoughts, feelings and behaviour that differs in significant ways from the culture in which the person lives. This pattern is pervasive and inflexible, begins in adolescence or early adulthood and causes distress or impairment.

Pharmacotherapy: Treatment of symptoms of disorders with medications that operate by altering the chemical balance in specific systems in the brain.

Postpartum depression: A depressive episode following childbirth, usually due to physical and hormonal changes.

Psychoeducation: An educational process that allows people to better understand and manage mental health and/or substance use problems, whether their own or those of a family member or friend.

Psychotherapy: A general term used to describe a form of treatment based on talking with a therapist. Psychotherapy aims to relieve distress by allowing a person to discuss and express feelings. The goal is to help the person change attitudes, behaviour and habits, and develop better ways of coping.

Relapse prevention: Managing a mood disorder by medication and/ or psychotherapy, or other supportive strategies to help the person remain well.

Transcranial magnetic stimulation (TMS): A brain intervention treatment that involves a series of short magnetic pulses directed to the brain.

Seasonal affective disorder (SAD): A type of depression that tends to be affected by the amount of daylight and the time of the year, usually occurring in the fall and winter.

Resources

SUGGESTED READING

Bilsker, D., & Paterson, R. (2009). *Self-Care Depression Program: Antidepressant Skills Workbook* (2nd ed.). Vancouver, BC: Centre for Applied Research in Mental Health and Addiction and BC Mental Health & Addiction Services. Retrieved from www.comh.ca/publications/resources/asw/SCDPAntidepressantSkills.pdf

Burns, D. (1999). *The Feeling Good Handbook* (Rev. ed.). New York: Penguin.

Centre for Addiction and Mental Health. (2002). *When a Parent Is Depressed . . . What Kids Want to Know.* Toronto: Author. Retrieved from knowledgex.camh.net/amhspecialists/resources_families/Documents/when_parent_depressed.pdf

Centre for Addiction and Mental Health. (2009). *Can I Catch It Like a Cold? Coping with a Parent's Depression.* Toronto: Author.

Coleman, L. (2012). *Depression: A Guide for the Newly Diagnosed.* Oakland, CA: New Harbinger.

Copeland, M.E. (2001). *The Depression Workbook: A Guide for Living with Depression and Manic Depression* (2nd ed.). Oakland, CA: New Harbinger.

Epstein, L. & Amador, X.F. (1997). *When Someone You Love Is Depressed: How to Help Your Loved One without Losing Yourself.* New York: Fireside.

Greenberger, D. & Padesky, C. (1995). *Mind over Mood*. New York, Guilford Press.

Knaus, W.J. (2012). *The Cognitive Behavioural Workbook for Depression: A Step-by-Step Program* (2nd ed.). Oakland, CA: New Harbinger.

Marra, T. (2004). *Depressed and Anxious: The Dialectical Behaviour Therapy Workbook for Overcoming Depression and Anxiety.* Oakland, CA: New Harbinger.

Mondimore, F.M. (2006). *Depression: The Mood Disease* (3rd ed.). Baltimore, MD: Johns Hopkins University Press.

Stahl, B. & Goldstein, E., (2010). *A Mindfulness-Based Stress Reduction Workbook*. Oakland, CA. New Harbinger.

Williams, M., Teasdale, J., Segal, Z. & Kabat-Zinn, J. (2007). *The Mindful Way through Depression: Freeing Yourself from Chronic Unhappiness*. New York, Guilford Press.

INTERNET RESOURCES

Canadian Mental Health Association (CMHA)
www.cmha.ca

Canadian Network for Mood and Anxiety Treatments (CANMAT)
www.canmat.org

Depression and Bipolar Support Alliance
www.dbsalliance.org

Family Association for Mental Health Everywhere
www.fameforfamilies.com

Mood Disorders Association of Ontario
www.mooddisorders.ca

Optimism (a mood charting app)
www.findingoptimism.com

Other guides in this series

Addiction

Anxiety Disorders

Bipolar Disorder

Cognitive-Behavioural Therapy

Concurrent Substance Use and Mental Health Disorders

Couple Therapy

First Episode Psychosis

The Forensic Mental Health System in Ontario

Obsessive-Compulsive Disorder

Schizophrenia

Women, Abuse and Trauma Therapy

Women and Psychosis

To order these and other CAMH publications,
contact Sales and Distribution:
Toll-free: 1 800 661-1111
Toronto: 416 595-6059
E-mail: publications@camh.ca
Online store: http://store.camh.ca

Printed in the USA
CPSIA information can be obtained
at www.ICGtesting.com
LVHW021931191024
794280LV00002B/483

9 781770 525719